American Farmers
and
The Rise of Agribusiness

Seeds of Struggle

American Farmers
and
The Rise of Agribusiness

Seeds of Struggle

Advisory Editors

Dan C. McCurry
Richard E. Rubenstein

THE

ALLIANCE·and·LABOR·SONGSTER

COMPILED BY

LEOPOLD VINCENT

ARNO PRESS

A New York Times Company

New York – 1975

Reprint Edition 1975 by Arno Press Inc.

Reprinted from a copy in
  The State Historical Society of Wisconsin Library

AMERICAN FARMERS AND THE RISE OF AGRIBUSINESS:
Seeds of Struggle
ISBN for complete set: 0-405-06760-7
See last pages of this volume for titles.

Publisher's Note: This book was reprinted
from the best available copy.

Manufactured in the United States of America

Library of Congress Cataloging in Publication Data

Vincent, Leopold, comp.
    The Alliance and labor songster.

    (American farmers and the rise of agribusiness)
    Reprint of the 1891 ed. published by Vincent Bros.
Pub. Co., Indianapolis.
    1. Labor and laboring classes--Songs and music.
2. National Farmers' Alliance and Industrial Union--
Songs and music. I. Title. II. Series.
HD1485.F24V55 1975   784.6'8'331   74-30660
ISBN 0-405-06837-9

THE

⊶ALLIANCE · and · LABOR · SONGSTER⊷

A COLLECTION OF

LABOR AND COMIC SONGS,

FOR THE USE OF

Alliances, Grange Debating Clubs and Political Gatherings.

COMPILED BY

LEOPOLD VINCENT,

INDIANAPOLIS, IND.

INDIANAPOLIS, IND.:
VINCENT BROS. PUBLISHING CO.
1891.

PREFACE.

(TO MUSIC EDITION.)

Ten months have now passed since we set forth to complete the Third Edition of this little Songster without the music. After its first appearance in the Social Circles of our great common people, the demand steadily increased to such an extent, that much of the time it has been beyond our facilities to meet. Over forty-thousand copies are now in constant use from coast to coast of our broad land.

Now, since its endorsement by the official bodies of the several great Labor organizations, we feel warranted in catering to the public wish by revising, and setting to music, as well as adding new pieces. It is with no slight degree of pleasure that we picture the thousands of people now singing *their own* songs, in the spirit of their own labors, and in their own societies.

Our poets have rhymed for the beautiful and wealthy, the authors have exhausted their skill to tickle the fancy of those who dwell in luxury and opulence. Our ministers have preached and prayed for the souls of men (too often after the pockets of the influential), and let the bodies go; but the single-handed farmer, mechanic, and day-laborer, has had to sing another's song,—if, by chance, he felt like singing at all after "duties" were done—or go without that music all men love, and nature craves.

It is for you we have issued this little SONGSTER, with a sincere desire that by its use your labors may be made more congenial, and with a hope that a condition may be ushered in, where the husbandman may in truth come home from his labors with song on his lips, and be met by the sweet sound of wife singing "Home, Sweet Home," in—not a tenement house—but their home indeed.

To those who have kindly shown such an interest to contribute choice pieces, we say, thank you. May this little book ever be a means of pleasure to all, and may the harmonizing influence of music have the effect of sealing the sympathies of our people till political strife shall be of the past, is the wish of

THE COMPILER.

SONGS FOR THE TOILER.

(REVISED.)

№ 1. Opening Song.

J. J. MARTIN.

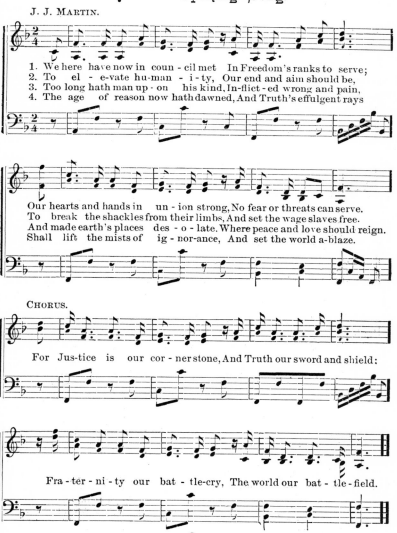

1. We here have now in coun - cil met In Freedom's ranks to serve;
2. To   el - e-vate hu-man - i - ty, Our end and aim should be,
3. Too long hath man up - on   his kind, In-flict - ed wrong and pain,
4. The age   of reason now hath dawned, And Truth's effulgent rays

Our hearts and hands in   un - ion strong, No fear or threats can serve.
To   break the shackles from their limbs, And set the wage slaves free.
And made earth's places   des - o - late. Where peace and love should reign.
Shall   lift   the mists of   ig - nor-ance, And set the world a-blaze.

CHORUS.

For Jus-tice is   our cor - ner stone, And Truth our sword and shield:

Fra - ter - ni - ty our bat - tle-cry, The world our bat - tle-field.

3

The Future America.

1. My coun-try, 'tis of Thee, Land of lost Lib-er-ty,
2. Land once of no-ble braves, But now of wretch-ed slaves.
3. Land where the wealth-y few Can make the ma-ny do
4. Land where a rogue is raised On high, and loud-ly praised
5. My coun-try, 'tis of Thee, Be-trayed by brib-er-y,

Of Thee we sing. Land which the Mill-ion-aires, Who gov-ern
A-las! too late! We saw sweet Free-dom die, From let-ting
Their roy-al will, And tax for sel-fish greed The toil-ers
For worst of crimes; Of which the end must be A hell of
Of Thee we sing. We might have saved Thee long Had we, when

our af-fairs, Own for them-selves and heirs, Hail, to thy King.
brib-ers, high, Our unpriced suff-rage buy, And mourn thy fate.
till they bleed; And those not yet weak-kneed, Crush down and kill.
cru-el-ty, As proved by his-to-ry Of an-cient times.
proud and strong, Put down the curs-ed wrong That makes a king.

3. Once More We Meet To Clasp.

TUNE—Above..

Opening Ode, No. 3.

Once more we meet to clasp
In friendships hallowed grasp
    The hands of men !
Oh, may our cause sublime
Throughout the length of time
In this, our native clime,
    Forever stand.

Patrons! stand by your cause,
Obeying Honor's laws;
    Move hand in hand.

No rich Monop'lies great
Nor foreign Syndicate,
Shall guide the Ship of State
    In this fair land.

Brave Sons, and daughters fair,
By Truth and Virtue heir
    To Honor's name;
Stand by your colors, pure,
And may your strength endure;
Reward, though slow, is sure,
    In this high game.

4

No. 4.   Awake! Be Free.

TUNE.   Page 4.

Our country, great and grand,
Is known in every land
    As Freedom's home;
Yet, through man's greed and lust,
Through laws the most unjust,
And from the giant trust,
    Great evils come.

Our liberties are gone,
Justice no more is done
    To faithful toil;
But want and woeful need,
From Mammon's reign proceed,
Which hurtful tumults breed
    And Freedom spoil.

How long shall we be slaves,
And bow to sordid knaves
    Who rob the poor?
Let every man awake,
And Freedom's weapon take,
The yoke of bondage break,
    And serve no more.

Great God of Liberty!
Through truth that maketh free.
    Make free the land.
Give us to see the light,
Lead us to follow right,
And show that *right is might*,
    By thine own hand.

Our country then shall be
A home for brave and free,
    And noble men
No landlord then shall reign,
To clutch the toiler's gain,
Our flag without a stain
    Shall wave again.
                H. W. FINSON.

No. 5.   Our Cause.

TUNE.   Page 4.

Our cause! it is of Thee!
Sweet Cause of Liberty,
    Of Thee we sing.
For Thee our fathers died;
For Thee we fight with pride;
For Thee we are allied,
    Thy reign to bring.

Through ages long gone past.
Through storm and bitter blast,
    Our Fathers fought.

Through foul and fair, and shine,
Fought they, the livelong time,
Fought they, in every clime,
    And not for naught.

From seeds that have been sown,
Strong-rooted plants have grown,
    And bloom apace;
Then shall we let them die
In their sweet infancy?
No! Let us strive and try
    To increase their race.

Now let us emulate,
The olden patriots, great,
    And stand for right.
Ne'er let us forget
The example they have set,
And when the end is met.
    We'll win the fight.
                CHARLES CHESEWRIGHT.

No. 6.   A New National Anthem.

TUNE.   Page 4.

My country, 'tis of thee,
Once land of liberty,
    Of thee I sing.
Land of the Millionaire;
Farmers with pockets bare;
Caused by the cursed snare—
    The Money Ring.

My native country, thee,
Thou wert so pure and free,
    Long, long ago.
Yet still I love thy rills,
But hate thy usury mills,
That fill the bankers' tills
    Till they overflow.

So when my country, thee,
Which should be noble, free,
    I'll love thee still;
I'll love thy Greenback men,
Who strive with tongue and pen,
For liberty again,
    With right good will.

And then my country, thee,
Thou wilt again be free;
    And Freedom's tower.
Stand by your fireside then,
And show that you are men,
Whom they can't fool again,
    And crush their power.
                THOMAS NICOL.

No. 7. To the Polls.

1. To the polls! to the polls! ye are thus serv - ing God; Let us
2. To the polls! to the polls! let the hun - gry be fed; To the
3. To the polls! to the polls! there is la - bor for all, For the
4. To the polls! to the polls! we will ral - ly a - gain; We will

fol - low the path that our fa - thers have trod; With the
ban - ner of life let the wea - ry be led; In our
king-dom of rap - ine and er - ror shall fall, And the
free our dear homes from the bond - man and chain; Then the

light of their coun - sel our strength to re - new, Let us
bal - lot and ban - ner our glo - ry shall fall. While we
rights of the peo - ple ex - alt - ed shall be, In the
home of the faith - ful our dwell - ing shall be, And we'll

CHORUS.

do with our might what our hands find to do. Voting on,   Vot - ing
her - ald the ti - dings *the peo - ple are free.*
loud-swelling cho - rus *the peo - ple are free.*
shout with the ransomed *the peo - ple are free.*

Voting on,

To The Polls.—Concluded.

on,   Voting on,   Vot-ing on,   Let us

Voting on,   Voting on,   Voting on,

work, and watch, let us vote, and trust, And la-bor till the vict'ry comes.

No. 8.   Opening Ode for K. of L.

C. S. White, Halsted, Kan.

1. Knights of La - bor, all fra - ter - nal, Meet we here for mutual help;
2. Hear the pleadings of the work - ers, As they toil from day to day;

Fine.

Guard-ed each by truth and just-ice, All our thoughts are not on self;
D. s. For the ones that hold the pow - er Rob us of our ev - 'ry need.
Let it be our aim and ob - ject To drive the hungry wolf away;
D. s. Ex - tend - ing to our toiling brothers, Ev-ery-where, a help-ing hand.

D. S.

Need-y bro-thers all a-round us, Suf-fer-ing from old Shylock's greed;
Give pro - tec - tion to the work - ers, Need-y ones all o'er the land,

7

No. 9. Storm the Fort.

TUNE. "Hold the Fort."

Oh, my brother, see the children,
Crying in the street,
Hunger's ravages revealing—
Weary, half-clad feet.

CHORUS.—Storm the fort at the election,
Hear the leaders cry;
Send the laboring men to congress,
With our votes, we'll try.

See the mortgaged, burdened farmer
Tremble 'neath his load.
Hear the mother's cry of anguish,
Families sent abroad.
CHO.

Fierce and long may be the struggle,
But our cause is dear.
Soon the laborers ranks will double,
Cheer, then brother cheer.
CHO.

Soon our banner will be waving
Up and down the street;
Laboring men have won the battle,
Victory's complete.
CHO.

No. 10. Our Battle Song.

TUNE. "Hold the Fort."

Hark! the bugle note is sounding
Over all the land;
See! the people forth are rushing,
Oh! the charge is grand.

CHORUS.—Storm the forts, ye Knights of
'Tis a glorious fight;   [Labor,
Brawn and brain against injustice—
God defend the right!

How the mighty host advances,
Alliance leads the van;
The Knights do rally by the thousands.
On the labor plan.

Strong intrenched behind their millions,
Sit the money kings;
Salary grabbers, thieves and traitors
Join them in their rings.

Vile injustice fills their coffers
With their blood bought gold:
And the might of their oppression
Ruins young and old.

Who will dare to shun the conflict!
Who would be a slave?
Better die within the trenches,
Forward, then, be brave!

8

No. 11.　Our Battle.

TUNE.　Page 8.

Hark ye laborers! Hear the sounding
　Of the battle cry.
Forward! Forward! To the conflict,
　Raise your banners high.
　　CHORUS.
Stand your ground till Victory crowns
　Strike for liberty!　　[you.
Use the ballot for your bullets:
　Strive for right or die.
　　CHO.

Break the chains of foul oppression;
　Bid the shackles fall!
Free the bondmen of the Nation
　From the debtor's thrall.
　　CHO.

Better prices for our produce
　We at once must have;
Also legal tender money,
　That we our home may save.
　　CHO.

Watch the candidates for office;
　Choose only good and true
Men to represent the people,
　And their interests too.
　　CHO.

Railroads, also, must come under
　Wholesome, wise constraint;
Syndicates and alien landlords
　Must yield to our complaint.
　　CHO.

Raise your banners noble brothers;
　Shout it as you go.
Onward! We will march to conquer,
　Out-voting every foe.
　　CHO.

Then we'll see our country thriving;
　Everything will bloom,
And the glorious light of progress
　Pierce our dismal gloom.
　　　　WM. T. EDGARE.

No. 12.　The Farmer's Voice.

TUNE.　Page 8.

Hark! the Farmer's voice is sounding
　Over all the land.
See, the Toilers forth are bounding,
　And the change is grand.

CHORUS.
Storm the fort, ye gallant toilers,
　Drive the Shylocks out:
Stand and vote against marauders—
. Hear the mighty shout

See the mighty host advancing—
　Justice leads the van;
Will you join the gathering millions
　On the F. A. plan? CHO.

Strong entrenched behind their lawyers
　Sit the Rings and Trusts;
Office seekers, thieves and traitors,
　Join them in their lusts. CHO.

Hark! the sound of woe arising
　From the Toiler's door;
Children starving, women crying;
　'Tis God's homeless poor. CHO.

Oh, how long ye toiling millions,
　Will ye bow the knee?
Arise, arise and join the Alliance,
　And you'll soon be Free! CHO.

No. 13.　My Experience.

Air: "Just before the Battle Mother."

Just before the battle mother,
　I was full of joy and glee,
I had hoped to marry, mother,
　And content and happy be.
　　CHORUS:
I mistrusted—yes mistrusted,
　That some one would get my due;
So, then, I investigated,
　And I found my fears were true.

A query now, I find within you,
　Asking me to tell it all;
It's the fight of life I mention,
　Of the toiling masses all.

We are asked to toil and labor,
　And to Shylock give it all;
I thought strange that we who labor
　Should be clothed and fed so small.

Shylock is a hard taskmaster,
　And I do not love his way,
For he has a mortgage plaster
　On the house I claim to-day.

Augusta, Kas.　　J. C. CLAUSE.

Fortune knocks once at every man's door, but she don't go hunting through beer saloons for him if he happens to be out.—*Puck.*

A modest little home, where love and affection abide, is the happiest spot on earth. When the poor, tired man returns to his home, after his day's labor is done, and is met at the door by a cheerful, loving wife, his cup of joy is full.

No. 14. Labor's "By-and-By."

TUNE—"Sweet By-and-By."

When the right over wrong shall prevail,
  And the woes of our people shall cease,
Then all trades and producers shall hail
  With a shout the glad triumph of peace.

  CHORUS.
It will come, by-and-by,
When the makers to manhood have grown,
It will come, by-and-by,
Then the age of true manhood shall dawn.

We shall sing on that glorious day,
  The melodious songs of the blest;
And our wives then shall sorrow no more,
  Nor sigh for the moments of rest.

Then the workers shall vote for themselves,
  And shall govern this land of the free;
The country, abounding in wealth,
  Will resound with true pleasure and glee.

No. 15. The Right Will Prevail.

TUNE—"Sweet By-and-By."

When the Workingmen's cause shall prevail,
  Then the class-rule of rich men shall cease,
And the true friends of Labor will hail
  With a shout the glad era of peace.

CHORUS.
  Right will reign by-and-by,
    When the Workingmen come into power;
  Right will reign, by-and-by,
    Then the gold thieves shall rule men no more.

Whatsoever men sow they must reap ;
    Since the rich to the whirlwind have sown,
More just laws they must now learn to keep.
    Then what Workingmen earn they will own.

Right, ordains that old parties must die
    And make way for the growth of Reform ;
Truth and wisdom proclaim from on high
    That the triumph of Labor must come.

Right on earth, evermore then shall reign,
    And the angels will sing once again ;
While the Workingmen join the refrain,
    "Peace on earth and good will unto men."

No. 16. To Our Homes We Go.

Closing Ode. TUNE—"Sweet By-and-By."

Gentle friends, all your duties performed,
    From the toils and cares of the week,
And from life's changing sunshine and storm,
    The sweet quiet of Home let us seek.
    CHORUS.
To our homes now we go
    By the sweet silvery moon's mellow light,
And the stars softly glow
    While we bid you a pleasant good night.

With our brothers and sisters to meet
    In the halls of the Patrons we love ;
All the friends of the Order to greet,
    But the hour bids us homeward to move.

Now may kind fortune's blessings expand ;
    May each honest endeavor succeed ;
May each true Patron throughout the land
    Be rewarded for each honest deed.

No. 19. Ring the Bells of Freedom.

TUNE—"Ring the Bells of Heaven."

Ring the bells of freedom! there is joy today
For a band that's battling for the right.
See the people meet them out upon the way,
Welcoming their weary, wand'ring feet.
CHO. Glory! glory! how the people shout!
Glory! glory! how the drums peal out!
'Tis the ransomed labor like a mighty sea,
Pealing forth the anthems of the free.

Ring the bells of freedom! there is joy today
For the vict'ry of each noble Knight.
Yes a slave is rescued from the birds of prey,
And the lab'rers hold the ransomed seat.

Ring the bells of freedom! there is joy today.
Sisters swell the grand triumphant strain,
Tell the joyful tidings, bear it far away;
Welcome all the true Knights of today.

My Country, 'tis of Thee.

S. F. SMITH, D. D.　　　　　　　　　　Dr. JOHN BULL.

1. My coun-try! 'tis of thee, Sweet land of lib - er - ty,
2. My na - tive coun - try, thee, Land of the no - ble free,
3. Our Fa-ther's God! to Thee, Au - thor of Lib - er - ty,

Of thee I sing; Land where my fa-thers died! Land of the
Thy name I love; I love thy rocks and rills, Thy woods and
To Thee we sing: Long may our land be bright With freedom's

cres.

Pilgrims' pride! From ev - 'ry mountain side Let free-dom ring.
tem-pled hills; My heart with rap-ture thrills Like that a - bove.
ho - ly light; Pro - tect us by Thy might, Great God, our King!

No. 20. Alliance Flag-ship Song.

TUNE. No. 1.

Oh, happy day we hail with joy,
Brave soldiers now declare;
Alliance flag ship comes, ahoy!
  On time's wide ocean fair.
All safe on board, the captain cries,
  To freedom's port we sail;
We'll take our foes all by surprise,
  O'er them we will prevail

Our ship is newly built, and strong,
  Our life boats all in trim;
And swiftly we do sail along,
  With soldiers full of vim!
Each labor party's a life boat,
  We've no great cause to fear;
O'er rocks and sandbars they will float,
  If wisely all do stear.

Though raging winds and foaming seas,
  Our ship may have to meet;
She'll plow through all with perfect ease
  And weather all complete.
All hail, Alliance Union men,
  Stand by your guns and fight,
For freedom and your country then
  You'll save in honor bright.

Let grace, and love, and truth abound,
  Ye toiling people all;
And may we cleave together sound,
  Nor from our Union fall,
What jubilees will then be ours,
  From want and slavery free;
Base syndicates and thieving powers,
  To sheol all must flee.

A government we then may claim,
  That's honest just and pure;
And a free people all remain,
  For ages to endure.
So may it be, great God of love;
  Cause equity and joy,
To reign below, as far above,
  Without the least alloy.

       E. D. BLAKEMAN. By per.

No. 21. The Orphan Song.

TUNE: "The Orphan."

"No home; no home," said the little
  girl,
As she stood at the rich man's door,
As she tremblingly stood on the pol
  ished step,
And leaned on the marble wall.

Her clothes were thin, and her feet were
  bare,
And the snow had covered her head,
"Oh! give me a home and something to
  wear—
A home and a piece of bread.

"My father, also, I never knew,"
And the tears dimmed her eyes so
  bright,
"While my mother sleeps in a new-
  made grave,
'Tis an orphan that begs to-night."

The night was dark, and the snow fell
  fast.
And the rich man shut his door.
With a frown on his brow, he scornfully
  said:
"No home, no bread, for the poor.

"I must freeze," she said, "upon this
  step,
As she strove to cover her feet
With her old tattered dress, all covered
  with snow,
Yes, covered with snow and sleet.

The rich man slept on his velvet couch,
  And dreamed of his silver and gold,
While this little girl lay on a bed of
  snow
  And murmured, "so cold, so cold."

When morning dawned, this little girl
  Still lay at the rich man's door,
But her soul had fled to that land
  above,
  Where there's room enough for the
  poor.
       Miss WINNIE JOHNSON.

No 22.   The Granger's Yankeedoodle.

GEO. M. WOOD.

1. Oh! Al and I went out to see The plowboys on their ranch - es;
2. And when one branch they'd mastered quite, They'd reach and get another
3. And so they formed a lit - tle band, And called it an Al - li - ance
4. They said the plan they hit up - on Put all men on a lev - el;

We found them in a sycamore tree, A studying different branches.
They said they's learned a thing or two That farmers all were brothers.
They strutted round like fighting cocks And bid the world de - fi - ance.
The men outside would nod and wink, And say "You'll play the devil."

CHORUS.

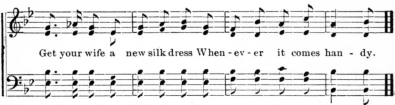

Yan-kee-doo-dle, farm - er John, Buy the bab - ies can - dy;

Get your wife a new silk dress When - ev - er it comes han - dy.

And now they sing another tune,
  And look amazed and wonder;
And say it's just as plain as day
  That things are "going to thunder."

And now the granger gets his goods
  Way down at bottom prices;
And pays the cash like money kings
  For all his little spices.

And now my little song is done,
  I'll bid you a l adieu, sir;
For Al and I went down one night
  And joined these grangers, too, sir.

16

No. 23. A New Yankee Doodle.

TUNE:—No. 22.

We toilers have made up our minds
To have a revolution,
And make "Perpetual Money" soon,
A standing institution.

CHORUS.

Yankee Doodle, banks and bonds;
Yankee Doodle Dandy;
Bounce the banks and burn the bonds;
Oh! Yankee Doodle Dandy.

We'll make the greenback crisp and new,
A lasting legal-tender;
Our simple votes can do it, boys,
For what is there to hinder?

When our bonds shall all be paid,
In lawful Greenback Money,
Our country, now impoverished,
Will flow with milk and honey.

Then proud will feel each workingman,
If he has done his duty,
And helped to crush the "Bulls" and
"Bears,"
Who care for naught but booty.

If we can only breast the storm,
And work and watch together,
The clouds will break, the sun will
shine,
'Mid calm and cheerful weather.

We'll pool our issues, brothers, all;
Lay down our private fancies,
For every sacrifice we make
Our victory enhances.

But, brothers, we can ne'er succeed,
Unless we are firm united,
With hearts and hands securely joined.
To keep the faith we're plighted.

Our mighty work is just begun,
We must not flinch or falter;
Each patriot soul must lay his all
Upon his Country's altar.

Capt. GEO. W. LOYD.

No. 24. The Farmer's Daughter.

TUNE:—No. 22.

Oh, here we are as thus you see,
Each one a farmer's daughter.
We know just when to legislate,
And when we had not oughter.

CHORUS.

So we won't have any of your banker's
sons
To kneel to us and bow, sir;
For we can do without a man,
If he can't follow the plow, sir.

The fifteen thousand that Armour paid,
To buy a legislation,
Was not the proper thing to do
In the face of an honorable nation.

CHORUS.

So we won't have any like Geo. A. Peck,
At Washington to loiter;
He schemes to work the farmer hard,
And swindle the farmer's daughter.

So, when we're hunting a candidate,
Oh, never do you doubt, sir;
We're sure to find a man that's read
How Peffer planned The Way Out,
sir.

CHORUS.

When brokers are freed from all their
harm,
And lobyists are dead, sir.
The banker'll bow unto the farm
And *come to us* for bread, sir.

17

25. Almost Persuaded.

Almost persuaded facts to believe ;
Almost persuaded truth to receive ;
　　Starve us a little more,
　　Masters, we thee implore ;
　　Closer the lines you draw
　　　　Sooner we'll see.

Almost persuaded dangers to brave :
Almost persuaded, misguided slave ;
　　Dare we our rights to take :
　　Dare we our chains to break ?
　　Poor, wretched souls awake ;
　　　　Soon we'll be free.

Almost persuaded, come, come today ;
Almost persuaded, fear not to stay ;
　　Changes are drawing near ;
　　Tyrants begin to fear ;
　　Join with us, now and here ;
　　　　Turn not away.

Almost persuaded, truth dawns at last ;
Almost persuaded, leaving the past.
　　Almost will not avail ;
　　Almost is but to fail.
　　Joyful the news we hail—
　　　　"Won o'er at last."

If you lie down, the world will go out of its way to drive over you; but if
you stand up and look severe, it will give you half the road, at least.—Uncle
Ezek.

No 26. March of United Labor.

TUNE: Page 40.

Come forth, ye toiling millions,
And join our worthy band
As on we pass to victory
To free our native land.
Our glorious cause we will defend
And equal rights demand,
While we go marching to victory.

CHORUS.

Hurrah! Hurrah! A shout of joyful glee!
Hurrah! Hurrah! We bring the Jubilee!
The farm and labor shall unite,
And sweep from sea to sea,
While we go marching to victory.

The lords of mammon tremble
When they hear our joyous shout
As on we press to victory
And put them all to rout.
The trusts and pools and money kings—
"We'll turn the rascals out,"
While we go marching to victory. CHO.

The toiling millions can't unite;
That's what the bankers tell.
But hark! the tramp of millions,
And their chorus, anthem swell!
They shout for home and country,
And mon-op-o lies' death knell,
While they go marching to victory. CHO.

We'll raise our fathers' banner, boys,
And spread it out on high;
Beneath these sacred stars and stripes
Mon-op-o-lies shall die.
We have the ballot in our hands—
All traitors we'll defy,
While we go marching to victory. CHO.

Our weapon is the ballot,
And our word is, "*Right about!*"
All hail the power in Union, boys—
We'll give the world a shout;
The hand is writing on the wall,
"Go, cast the devils out,"
While we go marching to victory! CHO.
GEO. CAMPBELL.

No. 27. Hymn to the People.

TUNE: Page 30.

Not to be alert with warrior strength,
To wield the sword or wave the glaive,
Or rise to conquer fame at length,
Proclaims the good or makes the brave.

To have the power to bide the scorn,
And rise above the hate and strife
Of those to wealth and title born,
Is the crowned courage of our life.

What are the swords that prop a king?
The farmer in his army's van,
The strength of soul that dares to spring
And show the monarch in the man.

Kings and the mightiest men of arms,
Strong as the heads of realms they bide
Sport as they may with Fortune's charms,
They are but leaves upon the tide.

In dim old sepulchers they lie,
The feast of silence and decay;
While the true world-heart beateth high,
And thrones itself upon to-day.

Give me the man whose hands have
tossed
The corn-seed to the mellow soil;
Whose feet the forest's depths have
crossed,
Whose brow is nobly crowned with
toil. C. D. STUART.

First of all we must heed the cry of the children. We must deliver them from the taskmasters and turn them over to the schoolmasters.—Edward Bellamy.

The real conquerors of the world are not the generals, but thinkers; the mind that evolves plans for elevating man, not arms that crush and debase him.

No. 28. The Farmers are Coming.

GEO. C. BEECHER.

1. Farmers now have grasped the handles Of ev-o-lu-tion's plow, And the
2. The men who sneer at "hayseeds," And steal their wheat and corn, Must
3. With ballots on their pitchforks, With Justice "to the fore," See the

soul-less imps of Shy-lock Can't stop their mov-ing now. They are
now all "go to grass", sir, "As sure as you are born." They, who
toil-ing hosts are coming Two hundred thousand score. Woe be-

bound to get from un-der Con trac-tion's dead-ly pall, That
soak the usurious mortgage, In base con-trac-tion fat, Must
tide the purchased min-ions, Of 'curs-ed old Mo-nop, Who dare,

CHORUS.

like the poi - son   u-pas, spreads Deso-la - tion o - ver all. Forward!
take a dose of   ex - pan-sion, And get a taste of that.
bar the way of   Free-men,   Or bid their columns stop?

all! Ye men of ac - tion! From Forest, Forge and Field; Leave be

hind, the men who fal - ter Leave be - hind the slaves who yield.

21

No. 29. Labor's Ninety and Nine.

Better sung as a Solo.

1. There are ninety and nine that live and die, In want and hunger and
2. They toil in the fields, the nine-ty and nine, For the fruits of our moth-er
3. By the sweat of their brows the desert blooms, And the forest before them
4. The night so drear-y, so dark, so long, At last shall the morning

cold, That one may revel in lux - u-ry, And be wrapped in its silk-en
earth; They dig and delve in the dusky mine, And bring its rich treasures
falls; Their labor has builded humble homes, And cit - ies with loft-y
bring; And over the land the Victor's song Of the ninety and nine shall

fold; The ninety and nine in their hovels bare, The one in his palace with
forth; But the wealth released by their sturdy blows, To the hands of the one for-
halls; But the one owns cities and homes and lands, While the ninety and nine have
ring, And ech - o a - far, from zone to zone, Rejoice, for la - bor shall

rich - es rare, The one in his palace with rich - es rare
ev - er flows, To the hands of the one for - ev - er flows.
empty hands, While the ninety and nine have empty hands.
have its own, Re-joice, for la - bor shall have its own

No. 30. Labor Free To All.

TUNE: No. 32.

Start the music, comrades, we'll sing a labor song;
Sing it with a spirit that will move the cause along:
Let it ring throughout the world in chorus full and strong;
    Now we are marching for Labor.

CHORUS:

Hurrah! Hurrah! Labor Free to All!
Hurrah! Hurrah! Hasten to the call!
Shout the joyful tidings, *King Capital must Fall*,
    Now we are marching for Labor.

Take the pledge to labor, friends. but after you have signed,
Put your trust in liberty, and work with might and mind;
March against the enemy, leave every fear behind,
    Now we are marching for Labor.

With Justice as our standard we are bound to win the fight;
Raise the Labor Flag aloft and shout with all your might;
We strike for home and freedom, for virtue, truth and right,
    Now we are marching for Labor.

No. 31. Marching Through Kansas.

AIR: No. 32.

The election now is over. boys, we'll have a four years' rest;
The promises that were given us, we happily will test;
And if they are fulfilled, boys, the party we will bless,
    While we are marching through Kansas.

CHORUS:

Come, boys, come! let's down Monopoly!
Come, boys, come! from bankers set us free,
And vote no more for lawyers, but farmers they must be.
    While we are marching through Kansas.

If I was a Republican I wouldn't try to kill
The blessings that are contained in a free coinage bill:
And the bankers up in Wall street had better now keep still,
    While we are marching through Kansas.

I think the time is coming, and it now is very near.
When the music of our farmers the congressmen will hear.
That something else we want, besides adjourning for the beer,
    While we are marching through Kansas.

Resolving and adjourning. consumes all their time,
Except what is spent in drinking of the wine;
While working for monopoly, they never waste the time,
    While we are marching through Kansas.

When we send them up to Washington. it's not upon their minds.
The duties they have found is of another kind.
To work for the farmers they haven't got the time,
    While we are marching through Kansas.

                 SAM BERHERS

No. 33. The People's Jubilee.

C. S. WHITE. *Copyrighted and used by permission of "The S. Brainard's Sons Company."*

1. Say, workers, have you seen the boss-es With scared and pallid face, Going, down the alley sometime this ev'ning, To find a hid - ing place. They saw the people cast their ballot, And they knew their time had come; They spent their boodle to get elected But were beaten by the people's

26

The People's Jubilee.—Concluded.

CHORUS.

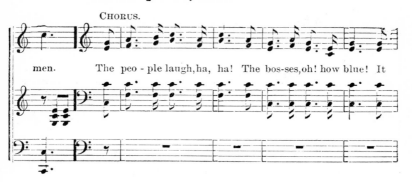

men.   The peo-ple laugh, ha, ha! The bos-ses, oh! how blue! It

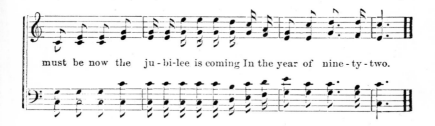

must be now the ju-bi-lee is coming In the year of nine-ty-two.

2. The bosses got to feeling so big.
    They thought the world was their'n;
  Of the starving people all o'er the land
    They did not care to learn.
  They blowed so much and called themselves leaders,
    And they got so full of sin;
  I 'spec' they try to fool the Almighty,
    But Peter won't let them in.

3. The working people are getting tired
    Of having no home nor land;
  So now, they say, to run this government
    They are going to try their hand.
  There's gold and silver in the White House cellar,
    And the workers all want some
  For they know it will all be counted out
    When the people's party comes.

4. The election's over and the rings are beaten,
    And the bosses have run away;
  The people's party came out victorious
    And have won the election day.
  They cast their votes for truth and freedom,
    Which are always bound to win;
  Up to the polls they walked like freemen.
    And put their ballots in.

27

No. 34. Alliance Song.

ALICE B. KENT.

1. Oh! Farmer, come and join our band, We'll gladly take you by the hand
2. Railroads now are all the go, Vote the bonds and they will show;
3. The day is drawing fast at hand When we'll wheel the mighty van;
4. At first we numbered ver-y small, But fast the farm-ers heed the call;

And do you all the good we can, For this is called a Freedom Land.
They'll build the road where'er they please, And now they're living at their ease.
Make Freedom ring throughout the land, And then we'll be a hap-py band.
From Texas' plain to Northern land, U - nit-ed now, we're bound to stand.

CHORUS.

Oh? Farmer, now, stand by your vow, Stick fast un-to your farm and plow;

Monopolies we must put down, And then we're bound to win the crown.

For e-qual rights we do implore: That's all we ask, and nothing more.

28

No. 35. The Kansas Fool.

TUNE: No. 34.

We have the land to raise the wheat,
  And everything that's good to eat;
And when we had no bonds or debt,
  We were a jolly, happy set.

CHORUS.

Oh! Kansas fool! poor Kansas fool'
  The banker makes of you a tool;
I look across the fertile plain,
  Big crops—made so by gentle rain;
But twelve cent corn gives me alarm.
And makes me want to sell my farm.

With abundant crops raised everywhere,
  'Tis a mystery, I do declare;
Why, farmers all should fume and fret,
  And why we are so deep in debt.

At first we made some money here.
  With drouth and grashoppers each
    year;
But now the interest that we pay
  Soon takes our money all away.

The bankers followed us out west,
  And did in mortgages invest;
They looked ahead and shrewdly planned,
  And soon they'll have our Kansas
    land.   C. S. WHITNEY.

No. 36.   Kansas Land.

TUNE: No. 34.

I've reached the land of corn and wheat,
Of salt, and coal and sugar sweet;
I got my land of Uncle Sam,
And am as happy as a clam.

CHORUS.

Oh Kansas land, sweet Kansas land,
As on its fertile soil I stand;
I look the pleasing landscape o'er,
For acres broad I strive for more.
Till Gabriel's trump, of loud command.
Says you must leave your Kansas land.

My chickens all are Plymouth Rock;
My horses Clydesdale Norman stock;

My cattle short-horns, very fine,
And Poland China are my swine,

And now at last the Alliance is here;
We've waited for it many a year;
And it comes to cheer the farmer's way.
And bring to him a brighter day.

EVA WEST.

No. 37. The Sugar-Coated Pill.

TUNE: No. 34.

We've formed a just and bold Reform.
  Yes, come, dear friends, aid the band
To rid our Nation of a curse.
  And for our Equal Rights demand.
    CHORUS.
Of Liberty, fond Liberty.
  What evolutions shall we see?
When honest Toilers take in hand
The Education of the land;
Then rally, ere the time has passed
To sway the "rod" from tyrant's
    grasp.

We used to be strong partisans.
  And tho't that we were always right.
While marching on to battle schemes
  Dishonest leaders laid to fight.

The party papers advocate,
  The theories of Plutocracy:
While superstitious ignorance
  Oft leads from True Democracy.

Yes, Party Politicians are
  As sugar-coated pills to face;
Then, having reached a sought for goal.
  Turn Tory to the human race.

They talk of Over-Production
  As if they thought we did not know
That middle-men, and lack of cash.
  Will hold the prices always low.

Republicans and Democrats.
  Just think the matter o'er and o'er;
You're being swindled by their tricks.
  So don't uphold them any more.
    E. Z. ERNST.

No. 38. A Wail from Mortgaged Homes.

TUNE—"While the Days are Going By."

1. There are sad sweet homes to cherish,
 While our days are going by;
There are mortgaged homes that per-
 While our days are going by, [ish,
If a home we can redeem,
 From the Sheriff's cry and scream
"Oh, the good we all may do!"
 While our days are going by.
REF.—Oh, they sigh! oh, they sigh!
 Oh, they sigh! oh, they sigh!
 While to home they say good-by,
 Hear their wail, "Sweet home,
 good-by!"

2. There are little children crying,
 While sad days are going by,
There are starving mothers dying,
 While sad days are going by.
Oh, the poor have only sighs!
 Tears that fall from weeping eyes,
 Help your starving brothers rise!
 While sad days are going by.
REF.—Hear their cry! hear their cry!
 Hear their cry! hear their cry!
 While sad days are going by,
 Oh, they sigh, "Sweet home, good-
 by!"

3. There's a time for holy frowning,
 While for bread our children cry!
There's a time for sacred swearing.
 While starv'd Fathers, Mothers die;
Oh, this awful curse and woe!
 Greed and gain alone bestow;
 Aching hearts! 'Tis so, 'tis so!
 While for homes your children cry.
REF.—Hear their wail, hear their cry!
 Hear their wail, hear their cry!
 Oh, they cry, "Sweet home, good-
 by!"
 While sad days are going by.

4. Oh, what vow is heaven asking,
 While such days are going by?
There is work for your God's demand-
 While such days are going by. [ing,
If your soul you can unite,
 In this God's great holy fight,
 Then the world will see your light,
 While your days are going by.
REF.—Do the right! all your might!
 Do the right! all your might!
 While your days are going by
 Stop that wail! "Sweet home,
 good-by!"   O. C. BROWN.

Close Up the Ranks.

TUNE—"Awake, Lady, Awake!"

The trumpet is sounding the call to the fray,
 To meet our oppressors in battle array;
 From the farms and the workshops we're gathering today,
 To close up the ranks, for 'tis death to delay.

CHORUS.—Let us close up the ranks, if we would be free,
 Stand shoulder to shoulder till the vict'ry we see;
 Then close up the ranks and we shall be free;
 Fling down the usurper, proclaim Liberty!

There are wrongs to be righted whatever the cost;
 Then get ready for action or the nation is lost!
 Our rulers are praising the gods of gold,
 While they banquet and bum like Belshazzar of old.

The strife between sections is passing away,
 And fraternal, kind greetings are exchanging each day,
 While the old party bosses are having their say.
 Since we've learned that we're brethren—the Blue and the Gray.

United, contend we for justice to all,
 And we've heard of the hand writing traced on the wall,
 By the finger of fate at the banqueting hall;
 We have weighed you, old bummers, and you're no good at all.

CHORUS (to last verse.)
 Let us close up the ranks if we would be free;
 Stand shoulder to shoulder till the vict'ry we see!
 Then close up the ranks and we shall be free;
 Smoke out the old bummers! Sound the glad jubilee.

S. P. REED.

This Southern Land.

AIR—"Beulah Land."

O, southern land, the farmers' pride,
No move its friends will e'er divide
When the Alliance rules the hour
And sweeps oppression out of power.

CHORUS.

O sunny land, my sunny land,
While foes oppress on every hand,
I look beyond time's stormy sea,
Where truth and right shall reign in
thee,
And view the people's happy shore
Of peace and freedom evermore.

The bitter past shall be forgot,
Sweet hope is made the common lot,
And north and south will each forgive,
And friends and lovers yet shall live.

The prophets of the days of old,
Who saw that rule of kings and gold,
Should meet a David in the way,
Would praise the Lord to live to-day.

Oh, cast away each traitor fear,
The jubilee is coming near;
And the Alliance is the plan
Of God to save this southern land.

C. M. B. Cox.

No. 39.   Oh! For A Thousand Tongues.

S. J. JOHNSON.

1. Oh! for a thousand tongues to sing The way our laws are used,
2. They walk the gold-en streets of wealth,And rise to luxuries high;
3. They will not heed our great lament,While they in luxury soar;
4. They tell us farm-ers to keep still—We must not speak nor weep;

In hon-or of our Money Kings, Us farm-ers to a-buse,
Us farmers who, in want or death,Can on-ly mer-cy cry,
They on-ly think of ten per cent, And how to yank some more,
In do-ing this their laws ful-fill And for our bread plow deep,

In hon-or of our Money Kings,Us farm-ers to a-buse.
Us farmers who, in want or death,Can on-ly mer-cy cry.
They on-ly think of ten per cent, And how to yank some more.
In do-ing this their laws fulfill And for our bread plow deep.

No. 40. Must be Something Wrong.

TUNE—"I've Found a Friend."

When earth produces free and fair
   The golden. waving corn :
When fragrant fruits perfume the air,
   And fleecy flocks are shorn,
While thousands move with aching head,
   And sing this ceaseless song :
  "We starve, we die ! Oh! give us bread !"
   There must be something wrong.

When wealth is wrought as seasons roll,
   From off the fruitful soil :
When luxury, from pole to pole,
   Reaps fruit of human toil :
When from a thousand one alone
   In plenty rolls along.
While others only gnaw the bone,
   There must be something wrong.

And when production never ends,
   The earth is yielding ever ;
A copious harvest oft begins,
   But distribution never.
When toiling millions work to fill
   The wealthy coffers strong,
When those are crushed who work and till,
   There must be something wrong.

When poor men's tables waste away
   To barrenness and drouth,
There must be something in the way
   That's worth the finding out :
With surfeits one great table bends,
   While numbers move along,
While scarce a crust their board extends,
   There must be something wrong.

Then let the law give equal rights
   To wealthy and to poor ;
Let Justice crush the arm of might ;
   We ask for nothing more.
Until this system is begun
   The burden of our song
Must, and can be, this only one,
   There must be something wrong.

No. 41.   The Runaway Banker.

TUNE—No. 33.

Say, victims. hab you seen the Banker,
  Wid de mustache on his face,
So 'long de road some time dis morning,
  Like he gwine to leab de place?
He see de smoke way up de railroad,
  Where de locomotives lay;
He took his hat an' lef' berry sudden,
  An' I 'spec' he's ran away.

CHORUS.
  De Banker run, ha, ha!
    De victims stay, ho, ho!
  It must be now de kingdom's coming,
    And de year of Jubilo.

De victims are so lonesome, libbin'
  In de sod house on de claim,
Da' move der tings to de Banker's par-
  For to keep it while he's gone.   [lor,
Dar's wine and cider in de kitchen,
  An' de victims dey got some;
I s'pose dey'll all be "resubmitted"
  When de Knights of Labor come.

De sheriff he did make us trouble,
  And he dribe us round a spell;
We lock him in de smoke-house cellar,
  Wid de key thrown in de well.
De club is lost. de handcuff broken,
  De Banker'll get his pay;
He's old enough. big enough, he ought
  Dan to went to Canada. [to know better,

No. 42. The Dawning Day.

TUNE—No. 33.

Say, Workmen, have you heard the
  Of the dawning of the day?   [story,
That shall light the path of those who
  And drive grim want away,   [labor,
Oh, Workmen. as we band together,
  'Gainst oppressors, high and low,
Let us widen out our magic circle
  From Maine to Mexico.

CHORUS.
  The toilers laugh, ha, ha,
    The idlers frown. ho, ho,
  Must be a real Republic coming,
    And the year of "Jubilo."

The toilers get so tired working
  That the nabob may enjoy;
They like not that the purse-proud idlers
  Scorn the poor men they employ.
They see the "trusts" lock up the sugar,
  And "tie up" the binding twine;
That the land is held by foreign la nd
  lords,
  So they say: "Friends, let's combine.

The "trusts" have given us too much,
  trouble,
  They have driven us round a "spell;"
But 'trusts' and 'syndicates,' 'grabs'
  and 'corners,'
  We will drive to death, pell mell.
The party lash we spurn forever;
  We have cast off the schemers' sway;
Our children shall march to life's long
  battle,
  In the light of a better day.

           EMMA GHENT CURTIS.

No 43. All Hail the Power of Laboring Men.

TUNE.—No. 39.

All hail the power of laboring men,
  Let the old parties fall.
Put out for candidates good men,
  And then elect them all.

We'll have congressmen who will vote
  For just and equal laws,
Repeal the bad ones we now have,
  And build up our cause.

We'll have for president some one
  Who'll help us all he can,
Who no bad deeds ever has done,
  And is not Wall street's man.

Let every voter in our ranks,
  For woman's rights cry out;
We need their help to down the banks,
  And turn the gold thieves out.

           O. A. McCOWN.

    The most solid comfort one can fall back upon is the thought that the business of one's life is to help in some small, nibbling way, to reduce the sum of ignorance, degradation and misery on the face of this beautiful earth.—George Eliot.

    Don't judge a man by the clothes he wears. for God made one and the tailor made the other.   Don't judge a man by his family, for Cain belonged to a good family.   Don't judge a man by his failures in life, for many a man fails because he is too honest to succeed.

No. 44. Brothers, Cheer.

D. J. STITER. *Copyrighted and used by permission of " The S. Brainard's Sons Company."*

1. In this or-der we have met, Brothers, sisters, brave and true, But de-
2. We have labored from the morn Till the setting of the sun, And our
3. Now, ye sturdy men of toil, We pray you lend your aid On the
4. There's a mighty work to do, Brothers, think before you act; To-
5. Down with salaries, down with fees; Fill our offices with those Who have

termined to resist old Shylock's power; And we have no time to waste, For they're
labor has the rich man's coffers filled; While the children of the poor, Beg-ging
side of Justice, Truth and Liberty; And our hearts will then rejoice,, When we
gether let us work in har - mo-ny, Till within our Senate walls They shall
Hon-est - y and Prin-ci-ple in view, May the toil - er in his might Scat-ter

watching I and you, And are tight-en-ing our fet-ters ev - 'ry hour.
bread from door to door, Till starvation has their trembling voices stilled.
see our shackles fall, And we hear the joy-ful cho - rus, "We are free!"
list - en to our calls; That indeed will be a glorious ju - bi - lee.
Freedom's bit - ter foes, And be governed by the loy - al, brave and true.

Brothers, Cheer.---Concluded.

No. 45. Temperance March.

(In memory of the Presidential election—1888.)

TUNE: No. 44.

1. At the polls to-day I sit thinking, politics, of you,
   And the homes that you are darkening every day;
   And I see men getting full spite of all that we can do,
   Though they try to put the liquor all away.

CHO. Tramp, tramp, tramp, the Girls are marching;
   Cheer up, rum, they have no vote;
   And beneath the starry flag they will see the suffrage go
   In a stream of crazy liquor down men's throats.

2. In the breech the faithful stood when its charge, corruption, made,
   And they swept us half a million votes or more.
   Those who stood to duty firm heard the cry all dismayed
   As Monopoly shouted victory o'er and o'er. CHO.

CHO. Tramp, tramp, tramp, the Trusts are marching,
   Soon they'll wear a Yankee crown;
   And beneath the starry flag we can beg a chance to live
   As we meet their approbation or their frown.

3. So within the Labor lines we are working for the day
   That shall come to enlighten all our race;
   And all honest eyes grow bright and all pure hearts grow gay,
   As they think of seeing home a happy place. CHO.

CHO. Tramp, tramp, tramp, the Girls are marching,
   Heroic in their efforts for Reform,
   Lest beneath the starry flag they will see the battle rage
   And their loved ones lying prostrate in the storm.

B. R. PERKINS.

No. 46. The March of Labor.

ISAAC JAMESON, Newton, Kas.

1. Come and see the Sons of La-bor ris-ing in their might and main;
2. I have seen them 'round the watchfires of ten thousand circling camps:
3. I have read that righteous judgment, and 'twas stamped with God's great seal;
4. They have sounded forth the trumpet that shall nev-er call re-treat;
5. Look ye now, the day is breaking, e'en the gloaming now I see,

Come and join in the pro-ces-sion, come and fol-low in the train,
I have seen them climbing mountains; I have seen them crossing swamps.
"As ye deal with my poor children, so with you shall justice deal."
They are sift-ing out the brave and true be-fore the judgment seat.
Shin-ing forth in a bright ha-lo that trans-figures you and me.

Let us haste the day Mo-no-po-ly shall
We may read their right-eous sen-tence by the
Let the he-ro, born of wo-man, crush the
Oh, be swift, brave hearts, to an-swer, and be
Let us put forth ev-'ry ef-fort, all hu-

cease his tyr-ant reign, As we go marching on.
great e-lec-tric lamps, As we go marching on.
tyr-ant with his heel, As we go marching on.
ju-bi-lant our feet, As we go marching on.
man-i-ty is free, As we go marching on.

36

The March of Labor.—Concluded.

CHORUS.

Come, ye brave, from ev'ry na - tion; All who're looking for sal-va - tion;

Come and join in the pro - ces - sion, As we go marching on.

No. 47. There Comes a Reckoning Day.

AIR: "Susannah, don't You Cry."

I had a dream the other night when every thing was still;
I dreamt I saw the lab'ring men all going down the hill;
Their clothes were rags their feet were bare, a tear was in their eye;
Said I, my friend, what grieves you so, and causes you to cry?

CHORUS.
    O, bondholders, take pity, now, we pray.
    We're out of food and out of clothes—
    There comes a reckoning day.

We have to work to earn our bread, and our children cry for food;
Have scarce a place to lay our heads, complaining does no good;
We hate to beg, we will not steal, pray tell us what to do;
We cannot starve—what shall we do?—we leave the case to you.

Our greenbacks 're gone, you've made us poor, reduced us all to slaves
You took our means, you took our homes, you've treated us as knaves.
We fought your battles, saved your homes, took greenbacks as our pay,
Now, when we ask for work or bread, you boldly answer, nay.

Bring in your bonds and get the cash the same you gave to us;
'Twas greenbacks then, 'tis greenbacks now; we'll end this little muss.
We must have money through the land, and business lively, too;
We'll feed the hungry, clothe the poor, with work for all to do.

You own the bonds but pay no tax, for justice now we cry.
You bought with greenbacks, now ask for gold; pray tell us how and why?
Who promised you to pay in gold? the people now inquire.
We'll keep our contract, you keep yours, as honest men admire.

No. 48. Equal Rights.

Mrs. Annie Locke, Tisdale, Kan.

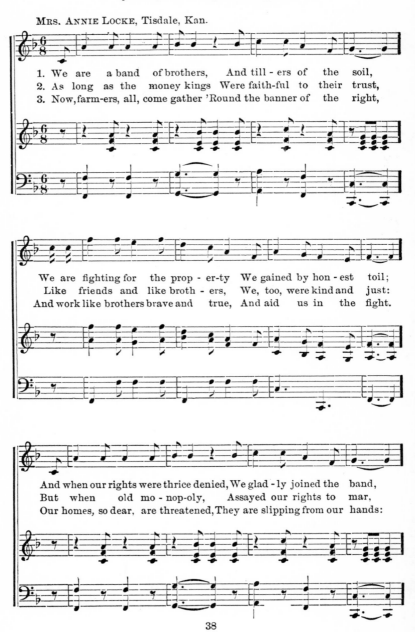

1. We are a band of brothers, And till-ers of the soil,
2. As long as the money kings Were faith-ful to their trust,
3. Now, farm-ers, all, come gather 'Round the banner of the right,

We are fighting for the prop - er-ty We gained by hon - est toil;
Like friends and like broth - ers, We, too, were kind and just:
And work like brothers brave and true, And aid us in the fight.

And when our rights were thrice denied, We glad - ly joined the band,
But when old mo - nop-oly, Assayed our rights to mar,
Our homes, so dear, are threatened, They are slipping from our hands:

Equal Rights.---Concluded.

And raised on high the Alliance banner, And for it we will firmly stand.
We raised on high the Alliance standard, And the cry arose near and far.
Then awake! awake! to in - ter - est work And join the Al-liance band.

CHORUS.

Hur - rah! Hur - rah! for e - qual rights, hur - rah!

Hurrah for the Alliance cause And the farmer's rights, hur-rah!

4. Then success to our grand Alliance,
    Oh, strong we are, and brave;
Like patriots of old we'll fight,
    Our homes from debt to save.
And in the coming years,
    Success will our efforts crown,
And the "grays," of other days, will be
    A people of renown.

No. 49. The Mortgaged Home.

OLD SOLDIER.

1. We   hear a   low wail-ing from close to the grave; The breeze bears it
2. Their mortgage is   cru - el, their hearts are but stone; They hear not the
3. Let us hasten,   my brothers, send forth the glad word, That Freemen are

on-ward; it   calls us   to save The   remnant   of   free - dom that
cry - ing, nor   an-swer the moan; The man   with his   mort-gage he
Free, in the   name of   the Lord! And will break the vile fetters that

has come to our lot; Yes, the birthright of home, to dwell in our   cot.
grinds us with scorn, 'Till hope spreads her pinions and leaves us forlorn.
now make us moan, And strike for the laws that will give us a   home.

Home! Home! sweet, sweet home, Yes, the birth-right of home, to dwell in our cot.
Home! Home! sweet, sweet home, Till hope spreads her pinions and leaves us forlorn.
Home! Home! sweet, sweet home! And strike for the laws that will give us a home.

"Love thy neighbor as thyself" has struggled for ages to become a law in human hearts, but as yet has failed of ratification by the people for universal application.—Better Way.

No. 50. The New Jubilee.

TUNE. No. 32.

Come, ye weary Laborers,
 We'll sing a glad new song,
'Tis the glorious Jubilee
 We've waited for so long;
Sing, then. as we never sang,
 United, firm and strong,
While we are marching to victory.
 CHORUS.
Hurrah! hurrah! another Jubilee!
Hurrah! hurrah! Deliverance we see.
North and South, and East and West,
Together sing with glee,
While we are marching to victory.

Many years we've toiled and worked,
 And wondered why it was
We were poor while others thrived,
 And now we've found the cause;
In unity alone is strength—
 'Tis one of Nature's laws—
While we are marching to victory.

Now we think as well as work;
 I'll tell you, boys, it pays.
We'll tend to our own business now,
 And do it our own ways.
Let old by-gones be forgotten,
 And work for better days.
While we are marching to victory.

"Now, boys, keep out of politics,"
 The politicians say;
"For you'll get hurt, or you'll hurt us:
 Don't meddle with it, pray;
Just work along, we'll tend to that"—
 Oh, tell us in what way—
While we are marching to victory.

No. 51. Onward!

Knights of Labor, onward ever!
 Cheer the comrades as you go:
Show the world by brave endeavor,
 That we'll triumph o'er each foe.

Knights of Labor, fear no danger,
 Shield the weak from every wrong,
Help the poor. assist the stranger,
 In your zeal for right be strong.

Knights of Labor, falter never,
 Boldly take a temperance stand:
Let our watchword be forever,
 God, and Home, and Native Land.

Knights of Labor, courage ever,
 Help your brother when you can,
And the power of wealth shall never
 Triumph o'er the rights of man.

Knights of Labor, see the morning
 Beams of light dispel the gloom:
And we hail with joy the dawning
 That shall seal oppression's doom.
 A. C. CALL.

No. 52. Nebraska Land.

TUNE: No. 34.

We're in a land of drouth and heat,
 Where nothing grows for man to eat:
The winds that blow with burning heat
 O'er all this land is hard to beat.

CHORUS:

O Nebraska land, sweet Nebraska land.
As on its burning soil I stand,
And look away across the plains,
And wonder why it never rains,
But Gabriel calls with trumpet sound
And says the rain has passed around.

The farmers go into their corn,
 And there they stand and look around;
They look and then they are so shocked
 To find the shoot has missed the stalk.
 CHORUS:

We have no wheat; we have no oats;
 We have no corn to feed our shoats.
Our chickens are too poor to eat,
 And pigs go squealing through the streets.

CHORUS.

Our horses are the broncho race—
 Starvation stares them in the face;
We do not live—we only stay,
 And are to poor too get away.
 JOHN A. DEAN.

No. 53. Keep them Burning.

AIR: "Let the lower lights be burning."
Brightly beams the farmer's vision
 From the dusty fields of toil,
For to him the Alliance giveth
 Rescue from oppression's toil.
CHORUS:
 Let the Alliance lights be burning—
 Send a gleam across the land:
 Some poor interest-burdened brother,
 You may help to save his farm.

Dark oppressions—night has settled
 Over lab'rers' humble doors—
Eager eyes are watching, longing,
 For the Alliance light to pour.

Trim your feeble lamp, my brother—
 Some poor farmer int'rest-pressed,
Trying hard to raise the mortgage,
 While old Shylock may be left.
 D. C. NASH.

No. 54. Looking Backward.

TUNE—"The Beautiful River."

Looking backward o'er the record the Republicans have made,
Can we still support their party with these truths before us laid?
First they put "except" on greenbacks, causing gold to take a
    rise;
But T. Stevens saw the danger, tears went streaming in his eyes.

CHORUS.

> We'll vote for the labor party,
> A good and reliable party,
> Vote to support the lab'ring party,
> That gives justice to all

Then they passed the national bank act, giving wealthy men the
    chance
To loan you money congress should do, and charge you high
    interest in advance,
Next, they contracted our money, and passed an act in '66,
Which burned up the national greenbacks on which the people
    paid no tax.

He who had a thousand greenbacks must invest them, if he'd
    gain;
But some enterprising business worked too hard his careworn
    brain;
So he makes a change with congress, takes an untaxed bond;
Congress now has got the greenbacks, in contraction they were
    burned.

The Credit Strengthening act comes next, which says these bonds
    must be paid
In the scarce currency of gold, and thus another plot was laid.
Then this debt must be refunded, 'twill not do to pay it yet;
Force it down on children's children, make them pay the enor-
    mous debt.

Yet to more contract our money, silver must demonitize,
Thus retarding a settlement, giving gold another rise;
Still they soon resumed the silver; but demolished greenbacks
    small.
Since they have so much deceived us, need we listen to their call?

No. 55. Labor's Chorus.

TUNE.—No. 44.

In the Labor ranks we stand,
Joining earnest heart and hand,
Seeking those who are in sorrow and distress;
Looking forward to the time
When the bells of Freedom chime,
Ringing forth the peal of Victory and Success.

CHORUS. Hail! all hail! ye Sons of Labor,
For our Cause is True and Just;
We are bound to break the chain
That is forging links of pain.
In our strength and wisdom toiling millions trust.

We are workers with a will;
We would in each mind instil
Noble principles, to form of life a part;
Then the future years shall see
Labor's Sons and Daughters free,
While a song of joy thrills every human heart.

Capital has had the rule,
Used the people as a tool;
But the time is coming when when this wrong shall cease,
For our army is strong.
It is marching right along
To the day of righteous settlement and peace.

E. A. BACON.

No. 56. The Alliance goes Marching On.

TUNE. No. 46.

The old parties are sick and laid away to die
The end of their existence is drawing mighty nigh;
To gain the people's confidence it is no use to try,
The Alliance goes marching on.

CHORUS. Glory, glory, hallelujah!
Glory, glory, hallelujah!
Glory, glory, hallelujah!
The Alliance goes marching on.

The old Shylock parties are so puffed up with sin,
We will dig a deep grave and drop them in;
They are so dreadful rotten they'd never pay to skin.
The Alliance goes marching on.

We will throw off the tariff, no time we have to lose,
And cheapen all the products the toilers need to use.
O'er the world by lightning will flash the glorious news
The Alliance goes marching on.

The grand old boodle parties are fading fast away,
The toilers of our nation will no longer be their prey,—
Looking fondly forward to that bright and happy day
The Alliance goes marching on.

The farmers and mechanics, as they greet the coming morn,
See plainly how the bosses had filched their wine and corn.
Now with united efforts a new party will be born.
The Alliance goes marching on.

C. S. WHITE, Halstead, Kan.

43

1. Old, venerable and time-tried party, Thou hast served us faithful and
2. Your actions were upright and honest, Both dur-ing and af-ter the
3. You're deaf to the wants of the masses, To the people you no lon - ger
4. "Small fry" would be swallowed by codfish—The codfish would slip down the

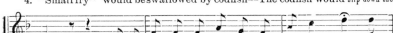

long; But the mal - a - dies you have been raising, For the
war; But the course you have taken of late years A de-
cling; Our bankers have led you to ru - in You are
whale; Honest men who have fought for the Un - ion Would their

peo-ple are getting too strong. We could once recommend you with pleas-
cent man can not but ab - hor; Your lead-ers, like A-bra-ham Lin-
run by the Syn-di-cate Kings. You are dai - ly becoming much weak-
homes and their country be-wail. You can no longer keep us in serf-

ure, And point to your record with pride; But Mo - nop - o - ly
coln, Have re-tired or been called a - way. Millionaires who would
er— The rea - son your leaders re - veal, That the rich man is
dom, For the people have opened their eyes; In the next Pres-i-

handles your rudder— All good things within you have died.
own our whole country, Have the lines and are driving full sway.
growing much rich - er— From the poor men your law-makers steal.
den-tial e - lec-tion We will give you an - oth - er sur - prise.

No. 58. Unlimited Gall.

TUNE. "Dennis M'Carthy."

My name it is Dennis McCartiz;
 I thought I would give ye a call.
I will sing of the darling old parties—
 There's no difference 'twixt them at all,
 The Democrats got into power by promises sacred and old;
But they crawled into the shoes of the Gentiles and the Jews,
 And the people's left out in the cold.

CHORUS.

Then hurrah! for the Demo-Republico party,
 With abundant, unlimited, cast-iron gall,
This great combination, to capture the nation,
 Is Monopoly, Whiskey, and the Devil, this fall.

The Republicans cry for Protection, the Democrats halloo Free Trade;
 You would think 'twas the Devil's own auction,
But the fuss that the blackguards have made:
 But when election is over, and the suckers have crawled into their holes,
Then the bosses will all take a notion to cross the wide ocean
 For a cargo of Italians and Poles.

There have many things happened this fall, sir,
 That fills us chuck full of surprise.
Sure, we'd never believe them at all, sir,
 If they wasn't so plain to our eyes.
Just see the Republican party; would you ever have dared to suppose
That they'd take our old flag, and make it a rag,
 And use it for wiping their nose?

[SPOKEN.]—In the language of Gen. John A. Dix. "If any man dares to
wipe his nose on the American flag, spot him on the snoot!"

The greatest sensation, they say, sir—
 It beats anything that we've seen—
The Republicans wear every day, sir,
 A sprig of the shamrock so green.
They will meet Paddy Whack on the corner;
 They'll take off their hats and they'll bow;
And they'll smile and they'll smirk, and their heads they will jerk,
 And they'll get in their work. and,
Although it is a sin, sweet Paddy will grin,
And straightway begin to rake in the tin,
And St. Patrick above us will look down upon us.
 And say how they love us, "O Lord!"

They have loaned out our money to the banks, sir,
 And they don't charge a cent for its use.
They call us an army of cranks, sir,
 Because we've found out this abuse.
And they all joined together like pirates,
 And fix up their company Trusts;
So they throw out their feelers to strangle all squealers,
And back up their heelers to crush out small dealers,
 These Demo-Republico Trusts.

They have loaded us down with a debt, sir,
 Three billions of interest we've paid;
And we will force this fact down their necks, sir,
 That not half the principal's paid.
Then they swell up and talk about honor,
 And tell what they've done for the cause;
But we raise objection to such rank deception.
 We will show them, next election, we're struck wid reflection.
They can all squeal Protection, but their Tariff injection
 Grows pale wid dejection. Be gorry, we'll fix 'em next fall.

The Republicans held a Convention;
 It was built on the Democratic plan.
There was whiskey too numerous to mention—
 Five gallons for every man.
They got up a great insurrection—
 Pint bottles and whiskey-jugs flew.
'Twas a hub-a-boo, bug-a-boo, Kilkenny cat-a-doo—
 Down the center and up the outside—
Gouge out your partner's eyes, pull out his hair.
 Mahone, of Virginia, got hit wid a chair;
Row-da-dow; what a row; wasn't it nice—
 The police came in and put them on ice.

[SPOKEN.]—Then they unanimously passed a resolution declaring that
they cordially sympathized with all well-directed efforts for the promotion
of temperance virtue, and morality, too.   C. M. MAXSON.

No. 59. The Alliances are Coming.

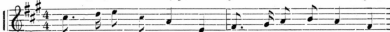

1. Don't you hear the ban - kers, Squealing o - ver yon - der,
2. A - way out on the prai - rie, In the state of Kan - sas;
3. Don't you see the peo - ple, Ris - ing o - ver yon - der,
4. It is the trusts we're fight-ing, And they be-gin to trem - ble,

Where the grand old parties congregate, But never you be frightened—
That is where they raise the corn and wheat; But the fes-tive mortgage—
Like they're going to have a ju - bi - lee; But they are on - ly go - ing—
They see us or - gan-ize the land; So they cuss the farmers,

They have lost their pow - er, And the Alliance, now, will seal their fate.
Robbed them of their earnings; And it left them scarce enough to eat.
To the Alliance meeting, That will shortly make them rich and free.
And they call them trai-tors, Because we raise them to a warn-ing hand.

CHORUS.

Look out there now! We are going to vote! Look
out there; don't you understand; The Alliances are coming! The
don't you know,
Al - lian-ces are com-ing! They are going to oc - cu - py the land,

46

No. 60.   Work, Work, Work, the Livelong Day

TUNE. No. 44.

In a hovel now I sit, thinking of the Days gone by,
    When I owned my farm, my house and my home;
But the mortgage on my Land took it all for its demand,
    And I sit and wonder where I now can roam.

CHORUS.

Work, work, work, the livelong day,
    Toil on from morning until night:
And I try to cheer my wife in the midst of all the strife,
    But I falter though I try with all my might.

In the front ranks we will stand, and will raise a warning hand
    To the ones who robbed us of our heritage,
And they best heed our demands and return to us our lands,
    Or we'll vote them down a hundred thousand more.

We are waiting for the day we can join in Freedom's fray,
    And will help to fight the revolution o'er.
So we'll throw dull care away with our poor hearts almost gay,
    When we think of having land and home once more.

C. S. WHITE.

No. 61.   The Battle-cry Of Freedom.

TUNE. No. 62.

Yes, we'll rally round the flag, boys, we'll rally once again,
    Shouting the battle-cry of freedom;
We'll vote the party-bosses out, we'll end old Shylock's reign,
    Shouting the battle-cry of freedom.

CHORUS:

Union forever! Hurrah! boys, hurrah!
Down with the bosses who think they're the law,
While we'll rally round the polls, boys, we'll rally once again,
    Shouting the battle-cry of freedom.

They may crack the party whip, they may bluster, they may brag—
    We shout the battle-cry of freedom.
They may even make a hobby of the resubmission nag—
    We shout the battle-cry of freedom.

They may try to win us back by a thousand subtile tricks,
    Shouting the battle of freedom.
But they've cheated us before and we'll send 'em up "Salt Creek,'
    Shouting the battle-cry of freedom.

They may beat us for a while, but we're gaining on 'em fast,
    Shouting the battle-cry of freedom;
God is with us for the right and we'll conquer at the last,
    Shouting the battle-cry of freedom.

FLORA M. JAMESON.

Any law which allows a few pampered pimps of mammon to put their
hands between the sweat of any one's brow and their mouth, is corrupt, and a
menace to good government.—E. S. MOORE.

47

No. 62. Our Watchword---"Union."

TUNE—"Battle Cry of Freedom."

We are springing to the ranks,
We are marching to the field,
  Shouting our watchword of "Union!"
We will strike blow after blow
Till the foe to us shall yield
  Shouting our watchword of "Union!"
    CHORUS.
Now, brother farmers, demand better laws,
Up with our standard,
  Defend our just cause ;
Let us never yield an inch,
Or from duty ever flinch,
  Shouting our watchword of "Union!"

We're approaching now a crisis,
And we must move with care,
  Shouting our watchword of "Union!"
We must choose to represent
Men who'll do and who will dare
  Shouting our watchword of "Union!"

Let us lower official salaries
And tax the moneyed throng,
  Shouting our watchword of "Union!"
Let our ballots speak for us,
Let them speak out good and strong,
  Shouting our watchword of "Union!"

Believe in "equal rights to all,
Special privileges to none,"
  Shouting our watchword of "Union!"
Work in unity together,
Do not leave one thing undone,
  Shouting our watchword of "Union!"
    CHORUS.
Then, brother farmers, demand better laws,
Up with our standard,
  Defend our just cause ;
Let us never yield an inch,
Or from duty ever flinch,
  Shouting our watchword of "Union!"

48

Song of Rebuke.

TUNE—"The Handwriting on the Wall."

At the gath'ring of the senate
  And a hundred banking lords
As they drank from champaign bottles
  As the record now records
At the time when they reveled
  In the royal white-house hall
Their eternal condemnation
  Was written on the wall.

  CHORUS.

    'Twas the hand of God on the wall,
    'Twas the hand of God on the wall,
    And their record is found wanting,
    They never can be trusted,
    And that hand is writing on the wall.

See the brave General Weaver,
  As he stood before the throng,
And rebuked the two old parties,
  For their mighty deeds of wrong;
As he read out the writing
  'Twas the doom of one and all;
Their eternal condemnation,
  That was written on the wall.

So their deeds are recorded
  There's a hand that's writing now,
They had better be repenting,
  To the Labor Party bow;
There's a day of retribution,
  It will come to one and all,
The execution of the sentence,
  That is written on the wall.

49

No. 63. Hurrah for the Toiler.

EMMA G. CURTIS, Canon City, Col.

1, Our fa-thers sailed a-cross the sea, In search of freedom true;
2. But now has come a hurt-ful power That like a can - cer clings;
3. Oh, sad to think this widespread land, Once freedom's pa - lace proud,

Their wealth was in their brawny arms, Their comforts were but few;
That nur - ses babes in filth and rags, And woe and hun - ger brings.
Should e - cho with such dis - con-tent As now a - ris - es loud.

Their hands were rough with honest toil, Their fa - ces dark with tan:
The food for which the far - mer delves, Smokes hot on the groaning board
Oh, haste the time when hon - est worth Shall sit in pla - ces high;

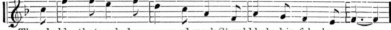

They held that each by some good work Should help his fel - low man.
Of one who neith-er toils nor sweats, Yet high he piles his hoard.
When ring, and trust, and banks that "bust" Shall hunt their dens and die.

CHORUS:

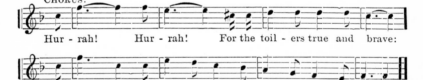

Hur - rah! Hur - rah! For the toil - ers true and brave:

Three cheers for the land so strong, That from want and hunger save.

No. 64. Sweet Liberty.

TUNE. No. 34.

Oh, will there ever law be given
For those who are to labor driven?
Who feeds and clothes this mighty land?
'Tis done alone by Labor's hand.

CHORUS.

Oh, Liberty! sweet Liberty!
Stamped on the banner of the Free.
When Labor, partly recognized
In social standing, then shall rise,
And side by side with Wealth shall stand,
United in one glorious band. [stand,

Oh, Brother toiler, lend a hand;
Oh, come and join this noble band,
And closer by each other stand,
And we can save this glorious land.

Money has ruled this world so long,
Too late, I fear, we see the wrong.
We are bound so tight by Shylock's thong,
Our power to save is almost gone.

Oh, Brothers, why are they so long.
In righting this most grievous wrong,
When all the wealth of this great land
Must be produced by Labor's hand?

The cry comes up from every land,
Arise, my brothers, loose your band:
You're held as slaves—oh, can't you see?
Now loose your fetters and be free.

D. J. STITER.

No. 65. Opening Ode. No. 2.

TUNE: No. 62.

We have gathered in the Order, gathered once again,
  Singing the joyful song of gladness;
We've resolved to be true, more knowledge to obtain,
  Singing the joyful song of gladness.

CHORUS.

United forever, we'll by each other stand,
Protecting the helpless all over this land;
Yes, we'll rally to our standard, so noble and so grand,
  Singing the joyful song of gladness.

With brave and honest daring we'll battle through this life,
  Singing the joyful song of gladness;
Protecting, aiding all, in this great and glorious strife,
  Singing the joyful song of gladness.

Let harmony prevail in all that we may do,
  Singing the joyful song of gladness.
We'll labor for the right, the good, the grand and true,
  Singing the joyful song of gladness.

NOTE.—Contributed by the Lodge at Assyria Center, Michigan; manuscript sent by Mrs. L. Dean.

No. 66. Music in the Air.

TUNE: No. 46.

There's music at the Capitol, there's music in the air;
We'll have music at election, too, and music everywhere.
The farmers are united, let monopolists beware—
  Our cause is marching on.

CHORUS:

Glory! glory! hallelujah!
Glory! glory! hallelujah!
Glory! glory! hallelujah!
  As we go marching on!

The Patrons are advancing, they'll be a grand success,
Reviled by all Monopolists and slandered by the press;
They scrape and bow to farmers for office now, I guess,
  As we go marching on.

They can not flatter Farmers by making false pretense.
Let us keep our eyes wide open and act with common sense;
Let us scan the records closely for the fellows on the fence,
  As we go marching on.

Let us work and vote together, with a due respect to laws,
Let us choose our ablest workmen to represent our cause,
Let us say to all monopolies, just loosen up your claws
  As we go marching on.

We have a Farmer Leader who presides with zealous care,
Whose rulings are conceded to be always just and fair;
Let us have him for our Governor, the first to fill the chair,
  As we go marching on.

We have looked the matter over and we know our cause is right;
We pledge but simple justice, to be noble in our might,
While we recognize the principle that might isn't always right,
  As we go marching on.

No. 67. Greenbacks the Money for Me.

Arr. by J. C. J.

1. My money is all out of pock-et, I'm poor-er than ev - er be - fore;
2. I've been in to see the old fel - low, Who's always claimed that he knew
3. He told me some things about money I nev - er had thought of before—
4. He told me a-bout the bond-holders, And railroad and telegraph men,

I wonder what can be the mat - ter— I'll ask the fel-low next door;
Why 'twas that the rich all grow rich-er, While poorer and poorer we grew.
It's all a cre - a-tion of fi - at, And made by our government men,
With lots more than I can't remember, I'm go-ing to see him a - gain,

He's always been trying to tell, But ne'er would I list to this scheme;
I listened, and listened, and listened; He talked thro' the whole evening long;
He talked of those National Bankers, And how to grow rich they had found;
And find some more about mon - ey And landlords who gets rents so high;

I've tho't him ex-ceed-in-ly craw-ly, For this is for-ev - er his theme.
I learned a good deal worth the knowing I've come home a singing a song.
They say, "We want gold.single standard." And gold is too scarce to go round.
And Shylocks who in-ter-est gath - er, Re-gard-less of pov-er - ty's cry.

CHORUS.

Bring back, bring back, Bring back my dol - lar to me, to me.

Bring back, bring back, Bring back that dol-lar for me.....

52

No. 68. Justice for the Farmer.

TUNE: No. 62.

From the hillside and the plain we have gathered to obtain
  Justice and freedom for the farmer.
We have hurried from the plow to demand and fight for now
  Justice and freedom for the farmer.

CHORUS:
  Hark! through the valley loudly sounds the horn,
  Down with the oppressors and up with the corn;
  We have set the ball a rolling, it gathers as it goes,
    Justice and freedom for the farmer.

Though the world the farmer feeds, many are his wants and needs,
  Justice and freedom for the farmer;
He must give the lion's share to the greedy millionaire,
  Justice and freedom for the farmer.

Must our yokes be always worn and our burdens meekly borne?
  Justice and freedom for the farmer.
Must we work with ragged knees that the rich may live at ease?
  Justice and freedom for the farmer.

Must we toil from day to day; must we wear our lives away?
  Justice and freedom for the farmer.
Let us struggle; let us fight; let us win, for we are right,
  Justice and freedom for the farmer.   LILLIAN SHAVER.

No. 69. Marching To Victory.

TUNE. No. 32.

Come join this great Alliance, boys, and march to victory;
Come put the Union armor on; from bondage you'll be free,
And join it with a spirit to conquer or to die,
  And we'll go marching to victory.

CHORUS.
  Arise! arise! your willing hands apply;
  Arise! arise! and swing the banner high.
  This shall be our motto, we'll waft it to the sky,
    As we go marching to victory.

See Giant Combination rising in our land;
The Trusts control our commerce, their leaders give command;
Then forward, Union Labor, and equal rights demand,
  As we go marching to victory.

Hear the voice of Congress, now; 'tis Tariff or Free Trade;
Monopoly rules the Government, the banker forms the grave;
You're swindled by the money sharks, we'll make the rascals fly
  As we go marching to victory.

Here comes the good Alliance Train—my God! 'tis just in time
To save poor wretched families from poverty and crime.
The headlight turned toward Washington, and steam-guage running high,
  As we go marching to victory.

Now keep the engine puffing, boys, and leave the narrow guage,
We'll run Monopoly from the throne, the Bankers from the stage;
We'll turn old Congress inside out, and set the Cabinet free.
  As we go marching to victory.   JAS. L. McCONNEL.

53

No. 70. The Banner of Freedom.

TUNE: "Hull's Surrender."

Come, all ye friends of labor,
    Wherever you may be;
Hoist the flag of Freedom.
    And proclaim your liberty.
Our fathers fought the battle once—
    I'm sure the cause was just;
We have got to fight it over,
    To put down rings, pools, and trusts.

We are marching against the money
    No time is to be lost,   [power,
We are going to have our freedom,
    No matter what it costs.
Our forefathers fought for liberty,
    And we must do the same;
To wear this yoke of tyranny
    Is a scandal and a shame.

We'll wage this war all o'er our land.
    And set our nation free!
We'll bear the toil, endure the pain,
    Till we're crowned with victory.
Then come, my noble toiler,
    And give to me your hand;
We will show them that the farmer
    Is able to command.

Come, all ye brave young countrymen,
    Girt on your sword and shield,
And march against monopoly—
    We'd rather die than yield!
See that you banish tyranny
    Wherever it be found,
And heal those bleeding farmers
    Of such a doleful wound.

Equal rights are all we ask,
    And those we're going to have,
If we'll stick to our integrity,
    And free those toiling slaves.
Then come, my brisk young farmer,
    Your motto, it should be,
When you march against those money
    Death or victory.   [sharks.

And when this war is over,
    And monopoly put down,
We will show that the farmers
    Are men of high renown.
We will send our men to congress,
    Who will make but wholesome laws,
And always willing for to work
    In behalf of Freedom's cause.

I have sung you these verses—
    I hope there's no offence:
I want you to peruse them.
    Especially those who are on the fence.

And if you lack for courage
    To battle with the brave,
Think of our forefathers—
    Never fill a coward's grave.

                        S. V. BABB.

No. 71.   Union Song.

TUNE: No. 28

Good morning, brother Union,
    Good morning, one and all:
We've left our home and business,
    To make you all a call.
We're around to stir you up, boys,
    To help you all we can;
To talk of farmers' rights, boys,
    And not the party man.

CHORUS.

For we've voted with our party,
    No matter what it cost;
We've voted with our party,
    Till everything is lost.
We have voted for our party,
    No matter where it went,
We have voted with our party,
    Till we havn't got a cent.

There was a politician,
    As we have often heard;
Who spent his time in spouting,
    To keep the people scared.
About his good old party
    He'd make an awful noise,
And use his party cunning
    To lead astray the boys.

There is a little thing or two
    That I should like to know:
When they've got our land and money,
    What will the farmers do?
We've neglected all advantages,
    And to the party stuck,
And followed after middle men,
    Till we are out of luck.

The youth is twenty-one, sir,
    And has a right to vote;
And don't you be induced to go
    Without your over-coat.
Then exercise your rights, boys,
    And never take alarm;
Yes, exercise your rights, sirs,
    And vote to save the farm.
                        R. J. MOORE.

No. 72. A Mortgaged Farm.

TUNE: No. 44.

Near our sod-house on the farm
We are working hard to-day;
　And we wonder when the better times
　　will come;
And our hearts so heavy grow,
For the mortgage we must pay. [home.
　If we have for our dear little ones a
CHORUS.
On, on, on, the day is coming,
　When the times shall better grow;
When monopolies must die,
And the Trusts must all break up,
　And we'll have no mortgage on the
　　farm, we know.

To this Western State we came,
When our hearts were light and free:
　And we thought the world we could
　　surely face;
But the times were very hard,
And no money could we see,
　So a mortgage on the farm we had to
　　place.

So upon our Kansas farm,
　We are watching for the day,
Which is slow, but most surely drawing
　near,
When for grain we shall get more,
　And the mortgage we can pay.
And we'll have a home for those we
　hold so dear.　Miss DOTT WEBB.

No. 73.　Kansas our Hope.

TUNE: "Red, White, and Blue."

Oh, Kansas, the hope of the nation,
　The first for reform is her boast,
To work for her own emancipation
　From all sorts of deals and their host
Of ringsters and so-called politicians,
　Who laugh at one being an easy dupe.
They may see we've changed our posi-
　　tions,
　When this fall they get left "in the
　　soup."

"Bleeding Kansas," they called her in
　war time.
　"Being bled" now the cry is far and
　　near.
We will try and keep pace with them
　this time
　And make all their "rings" disappear.
In the fall when our crops shall have
　ripened
　And gathered, and safe from their
　　grasp,
Let us see that our future is brightened,
　And give to these sharks their last gasp.

Then gird on your armor for action,
　And see that your ballot is true.
Let no Demo-Republico faction
　Make you think all they thought of,
　　was you,
And they voted for "trusts" and "com-
　．binations,"
　To steal all you worked for so long.
Let them know (if its any consolation)
　That we now intend to right this foul
　　wrong.

Hurrah! then for Kansas forever,
　May she ever be first in the van.
"Let us lead, never follow," be ever
　The motto of each Kansas man.
With her "Knights of Labor" and "Al-
　liance."
　To uphold her principles of right. [ance
We will then bid all "combines" defi-
　And be strong in our faith and our
　　might.　Mrs. HATTIE V. BELDIN.

No. 74.　Are You Going to Vote Aright.

AIR: Are You Going Home To-night.

Election day is coming,
　November's near at hand;
Gird on your armor, farmers,
　And make a sturdy stand.
Will you vote for home and country,
　And keep your record white?
Will you vote for Labor's honor?
　Are you going to vote aright?
CHORUS.
　Are you going to vote aright?
　Are you going to vote aright?
Will you vote against monopoly,
　And make a gallant fight
'Gainst the power of cliques and rings
　That have proved the nation's blight?
On the fourth of next November
　Are you going to vote aright?

We've waited long for aid
　That is promised every year;
Our spirits have grown faint,
　And our hearts are filled with fear.
We've lost all hope of help,
　And are searching for the light—
In the ballot box we'll find it
　If all laborers vote aright.

The ballot box is mighty,
　It rules o'er all the land;
You hold the nation's safety
　Within your good right hand;
Will you use that power wisely,
　And work with all your might
To save our glorious country?
　Are you going to vote aright?
　　　　CLARA M. EGAN.

The Hope of the Nation.

B. W. GOODHUE.

1. The greenback, the hope of the nation, The money the peo-ple de-
2. When War raged in madness and fury, And bankers their mon-ey de-
3. The greenback, the peoples cre-a-tion, The money for rich and for

mand; It saved us from war's des-o-la-tion, And
nied, It came like an an-gel of mer-cy, And
poor, Will u-nite all the states of our na-tion In

shall be supreme in the land. May the friends of the cause be u-
guid-ed our ship o'er the tide. It gave us both sail-ors and
heart and in hand as of yore. It will o-pen the workshop and

56

The Hope of the Nation.—Concluded.

nited,   Like an ar - my march on to the fight,   Till the wrongs of the
soldiers When Lib - er - ty's wounds were in view;   It scatter'd the
foundry,   Many snips it will send from our shore; It will bless ev-'ry

wrong'd are all righted   And   ty-rants shall wail in their flight.
hordes of in - tru-ders, And   honored the brave and the true.
home in the country.   And   save us from tramps by the score.

Chorus.

And tyrants shall wail in their flight, And tyrants shall wail in their flight,
And honored the brave and the true, And honored the brave and the true,
And save us from tramps by the score, And save us from tramps by the score,

Till the wrongs of the wrong'd are all righted, And tyrants shall wail in their flight.
It scattered the hordes of intruders, And honored the brave and the true.
It will bless ev'ry home in the country, And save us from tramps by the score.

57

No. 76. In God let us Repose.

TUNE: No. 48.

Ho freedom's sun is rising, and shining bright and clear,
Take heart ye toiling millions, no longer doubt or fear;
Arise with power and might now, give battle to our foes;
The horrison is clearing, in God let us repose.

CHORUR. Hurrah, hurrah! united we will stand,
And the oppressors power, take boldly from his hand.

Together we are marching, a host of brothers true,
We mean to take the goal too, for that is our just due,
We've suffered now too long though, from syndicates and rings,
No longer should we pay them two prices for all things.

Henceforth cooperation, our motto word should be,
And what we earn we've right to, that fact we all can see;
Come leave the rotten hulks now, ye discontented crews,
The Union Labor ticket, can make us "rich as Jews."

What is the use to labor and sweat day in, day out;
To support the greedy sharks, which thing we've been about,
They get their heads together, and plan to cheat us all,
No matter what we suffer; but justice now doth call.

No fusing with the "mugwumps," demo-republicans;
They're doomed to desolation, with all their wicked plans.
Stand firmly, close united, all ye who would obtain.
Your liberty from tyrants, in this our wide domain.

Our wrongs must all be righted, for justice cries aloud,
Iron will and courage, will rout the thieving crowd;
All vote the peoples ticket, its for the loyal host
And it must be supported, let what may be the cost.

ELISHA D. BLAKEMAN, Three Rivers, Mich.

No. 77. Rally to the Call, Boys.

TUNE: No. 62.

Let us rally to the call, boys, rally to the call,
Shouting the battle-cry of Freedom!
We're determined that the rule of oppression now must fall,
Shouting the battle-cry of Freedom!

CHORUS. The Workingmen forever. Hurrah, boys, hurrah!
Down with oppression, demand equal laws.
So we'll rally to the call, boys, rally once again,
Shouting the battle-cry of Freedom.

We are coming from the East, we are coming from the West,
Shouting the battle-cry of Freedom!
All monopolies we'll hurl from their hold, too long possessed,
Shouting the battle-cry of Freedom!

Our Country stands in danger, and calls for volunteers;
Come, with the battle-cry of Freedom!
To burst the bonds of gold, boys, let us persevere
Shouting the battle-cry of Freedom!

"In Unity is Strength," boys, then bravely march along,
Shouting the battle-cry of Freedom!
Lay old party ties aside, and for equal rights be strong
Shouting the battle-cry of Freedom!

No. 78. The Poor Married Man.

Ballad.

You may tell of the joys of the sweet honeymoon,
    I'll agree they are nice while they last;
But in most every case they are over too soon,
    And are counted as things of the past.
The troubles and trials are sure to begin,
    Though you may do all that you can;
You'll wish you were out of the clatter and din
    That follows the poor married man.

CHORUS: With the trouble and fuss, the racket and muss,
    His face has grown haggard and wan;
You can tell by his clothes, wherever he goes,
    That he is a poor married man.

He works all the day, and tries to be gay,
    Forgetting his worry and care;
He whistles it down as he goes through the town,
    Though his heart may be full of despair,
For his very last cent must be paid out for rent,
    While at home there is Mollie and Dan,
Both crying for shoes it gives him the blues,
    To think he's a poor married man.

When he goes to his bed and his poor tired head
    He lays on the edge of a rail,
And the colic and croup make him jump up and whoop
    Like a dog with a can to his tail.
He must rock, he must walk, he must sing, he must talk,
    He must run for the water and fan,
He must bounce, he must leap, he must do without sleep
    If he is a poor married man.

From his mother-in-law he gets nothing but jaw,
    No matter how hard he may try
To keep her in trim, for she'll light into him
    And all of his wishes defy.
He's a fool and a brute, and he never can suit,
    Though he does just the best he can.
He had better be dead, for it then can be said,
    He's at rest now, the poor married man.

No. 79. Coming By-and-by.

AIR—Coming By-and-by.

A better day is coming, a morning promised long
When girded right, with holy might, will overthrow the wrong;
When God, the Lord, will listen to every plaintive sigh,
And stretch His hand o'er every land, with Justice, by-and-by.

CHORUS. Coming by-and-by, coming by-and-by!
    The better day is coming, the morning draweth nigh;
Coming by-and-by, coming by-and-by!
    The welcome dawn will hasten on, 'tis coming by-and-by.

The boast of haughty Error no more will fill the air,
But age and youth will love the truth, and spread it everywhere;
No more from want and sorrow will come the hopeless cry,
And strife will cease, and perfect peace will flourish by-and-by.

Oh! for that welcome dawning, when happiness and peace
Shall bless the land from east to west, and suffering shall cease;
This glorious consummation our principles will bring,
Then plenty will our homes all fill; its coming; let us sing.

No. 80. Good-bye, Old Party, Good-bye.

C. S. White.

1. It was no more than a year a - go, Good-bye, old party. good-bye.
2. I was often scourged with the party lash, Good-bye, old party, good-bye.
3. I was raised up in the kind of school, Good-bye, old party, good-bye.
4. The old party is on the downward track, Good-bye, old party, good-bye.

That I was in love with my par - ty so, Good-bye, old party, good-bye.
The boss - es laid on with demands for cash; Good-bye, old party, good-bye.
That taught to bow to mon - ey rule, Good-bye, old party, good-bye.
Pick-ing his teeth with a tar - iff tack, Good-bye, old party, good-bye.

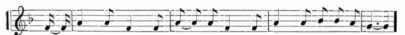

To hear aught else I never would go; Good-bye, old party, good-bye.
To do aught else I deemed it rash, Good-bye, old party, good-bye.
And it made of me a "Kan-sas Fool," Good-bye, old party, good-bye.
With a placard pinned up - on its back, Good-bye, old party, good-bye.

Like all the rest I made a great blow, Good-bye, old party, good-bye.
So I had to take it. or lose my hash, Good-bye, old party, good-bye.
When they found I was a will-ing tool, Good-bye, old party, good-bye.
That plainly states, "I will never come back, Good-bye, old party, good-bye.

Chorus.

Bye, par - ty, bye, lo; bye, par - ty, bye, lo;

Bye, par-ty, bye, lo; good-bye, old par - ty, good - bye.

60

No. 81. Paddle their own Canoe.

TUNE: "Joe Bowers."

My name it is Pat Murphy,
I live on what I can;
I spent the best part of me life
In serving Uncle Sam.
I've heard the rebel bullets whiz
When Dixey's land I roamed;
But I didn't know they were plotting
To rob me of my home. [then

I've voted for the good old P.
Just like a little man.
I hated all the Democrats
Like all Republicans.
They kept me hot a good long time
In throwing up their dirt;
And oh, my God, how mad I got
To see the bloody shirt.

And just before election day
Their papers were all filled [South
With news, they claimed, just from the
Of many niggers killed.
And then their boodle candidates
Were sure of their success:
The mortgaged home you live on
Will tell to you the rest.

Sure as Pat Murphy is my name
I've learned a thing or two;
The Farmers must all get in line
And paddle their own canoe.
For if they stick to party love,
And try to make it win,
Bedads, the devil will get us all,
And get us ready skinned.
S. T. JOHNSON.

No. 82. The Light is Breaking.

TUNE: "The Morning Light is Breaking.

The glorious light is breaking,
The darkness flies away,
The people are awak'ning
To see a brighter day.
From ev'ry hill and valley
Thro'out earth's wide domain,
The friends of Labor rally
To break the tyrant's reign.

The Knighthood's trump is sounding,
Its echos roll along.
By hundreds and by thousands
The people join the song.
Now joyous acclamations
Come rising on the gale;
No more with lamentations,
For people will prevail.

No. 83. Dear Brother.

TUNE. Gospel Hymn 240.

Why do you wait dear brother?
Why cling to ould Party so strong?
They have doen nothing to aid you,
Though they've been in power so long.
CHORUS.
||:Why not! Why not!
Why not come to us now?:||

What do you hope for dear brother?
What, the reward at last? [ture
Doe you think they will aid you in fu-
Any more than they have in the past.

Do you not feel dear brother
That old parties are going astray?
Then, why not join our Union
And help check monoplies sway.

Oh! do not wail dear brother,
The time is passing away—
A mortgage is due on the homestead,
Which the banker will call for some day

The lawyers will tell you dear brother,
That the nation can't run without
And you must vote with old paries [brain
And stand with the gamblers of grain.

But history tells us dear brother,
That Englands oppressive hand
Forced our toiling Fore-fathers,
To make the grand laws of our land.

84. When Workingmen Combine.

TUNE. No. 1.

Should song and music be forgot
When workingmen combine?
With love united may they not
Have power almost divine?
CHORUS:
The workingmen are free to choose,
The workingmen are free;
The brotherhood are bound to show
That workingmen are free.

Shall those who raise the fruits and
Who feed and clothe the race, [grains
Tramp through the land and for their
Starve, branded with disgrace. [pains

Shall banks and railroad kings unite
For base and selfish ends?
And those who labor for the right
Prove false, and not true friends?

Shall idle drones still live like kings
On labor not their own, [rings
While true men starve, and thieves and
Reap where they have not sown?

No. 85. My Party Led Me.

S. T. JOHNSON, Trivoli, Kan.

1. All the way my par-ty led me, And they robbed me ev-'ry day;
2. All the way my par-ty led me, And these wrongs I helped to make;
3. All the way my par-ty led me, I was blind and could not see.
4. All the way my par-ty led me, Led me to the fix I'm in;

But I did not see my fol - ly Till my home was took a - way.
For the Dem - o-crats I hat - ed, When the bloody shirt they'd shake.
When I hallowed and I shout-ed O - ver par - ty vic-tor - y,
But I will no lon-ger heed them, A new life I'll now be - gin.

Mortgage farmers, wives and children, Ral-ly to the Alliance call,
Oh! how true did Abe, the pro-phet, Tell us of this troubled day!
In our vic - to - ry was de - feat, As we now can plain-ly see,
O yes, farm-ers, day is breaking, Scales now from our eyes do fall;

For, if you should longer tar - ry, Money kings will have it all.
How the mon-ey kings would rob us, Take our lib - er - ties a - way.
For we're on the road to slave - ry, And must fight if we'd be free.
For we see the great in - just - ice That's been done to one and all.

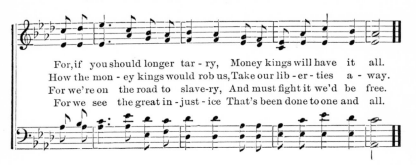

For, if you should longer tar - ry, Money kings will have it all.
How the mon - ey kings would rob us, Take our lib - er - ties a - way.
For we're on the road to slave-ry, And must fight it we'd be free.
For we see the great in - just - ice That's been done to one and all.

No. 86. The Bondholder and the Soldier.

TUNE: "Susannah."

"The times are hard!" the people cry;
   "We have no work or bread;
Our humble homes are swept away
   From o'er our children's head."

CHORUS: O bondholder! fear you no wrath divine?
That humble and peaceful home,
Bondholder, once was mine.

To win that home I bared my arm,
   I breasted many a storm;
My lovely wife, too, lost her health
   And bowed her lovely form.

CHORUS: O bondholder! by stars that o'er me shine,
That humble home you robbed me of
Shall soon again be mine!

You sent me out to meet the foe
   And staid yourself behind,
And while you rolled in splendor grand
   I long in prison pined.

CHORUS: O bondholder! don't think me so supine,
The greenbacks that you paid me then
Shall surely now be mine!

We met the foe on many fields
   And drove them to the sea;
We thought the Union then was saved
   And all our people free.

CHORUS: O bondholder! fear you no wrath divine?
The blows we dealt on Southern heads
Shall surely fall on thine.

INDEX.

American Farmers
and
The Rise of Agribusiness

Seeds of Struggle

An Arno Press Collection

Allen, Ruth Alice. **The Labor of Women in the Production of Cotton.** 1933

Bailey, L[iberty] H[yde]. **Cyclopedia of American Agriculture.** Vol. II: Crops. 1912

Bankers and Beef. 1975

[Bivins, Frank Jarris]. **The Farmer's Political Economy.** 1913

Blumenthal, Walter Hart. **American Indians Dispossessed.** 1955

Brinton, J. W. **Wheat and Politics.** 1931

Caldwell, Erskine and Margaret Bourke-White. **You Have Seen Their Faces.** 1937

Cannery Captives. 1975

Children in the Fields. 1975

The Commission on Country Life. **Report of the Commission on Country Life.** 1911

The Co-operative Central Exchange. **The Co-operative Pyramid Builder.** three vols. July 1926-January 1931

Dies, Edward Jerome. **The Plunger:** A Tale of the Wheat Pit. 1929

Dunning, N. A. **The Farmers' Alliance History and Agricultural Digest.** 1891

Everitt, J[ames] A. **The Third Power:** Farmers to the Front. 1907

The Farmer-Labor Party—History, Platform and Programs. 1975

Greeley, Horace. **What I Know of Farming.** 1871

Hill, John, Jr. **Gold Bricks of Speculation.** 1904

Howe, Frederic C. **Privilege and Democracy in America.** 1910

James, Will. **Cowboys North and South.** 1924

Kerr, W[illiam] H[enry]. **Farmers' Union and Federation Advocate and Guide.** 1919

King, Clyde L. **Farm Relief.** 1929

Kinney, J. P. **A Continent Lost—A Civilization Won.** 1937

Land Speculation: New England's Old Problem. 1975

Lange, Dorothea and Paul Schuster Taylor. **An American Exodus:** A Record of Human Erosion. 1939

Lord, Russell. **Men of Earth.** 1931

Loucks, H[enry] L. **The Great Conspiracy of the House of Morgan and How to Defeat It.** 1916

Murphy, Jerre C. **The Comical History of Montana.** 1912

The National Nonpartisan League Debate. 1975

Orr, James L. **Grange Melodies.** 1911

Proctor, Thomas H. **The Banker's Dream.** 1895

Rochester, Anna. **Why Farmers Are Poor.** 1940

Russell, Charles Edward. **The Greatest Trust in the World.** 1905

Russell, Charles Edward. **The Story of the Nonpartisan League.** 1920

Simons, A. M. **The American Farmer.** 1902

Simonsen, Sigurd Jay. **The Brush Coyotes.** 1943

Todes, Charlotte. **Labor and Lumber.** 1931

U. S. Department of Labor. **Labor Unionism in American Agriculture.** 1945

U. S. Federal Trade Commission. **Cooperative Marketing.** 1928

U. S. Federal Trade Commission. **Report of the Federal Trade Commission on Agricultural Income Inquiry.** 1938. three vols. in two

U. S. Senate Committee on Education and Labor. **Violations of Free Speech and Rights of Labor.** 1941. three vols. in one

Vincent, Leopold. **The Alliance and Labor Songster.** 1891

Wallace, Henry C. **Our Debt and Duty to the Farmer.** 1925

Watson, Thomas E. **The People's Party Campaign Book.** [1893]

[White, Roland A.]. **Milo Reno, Farmers Union Pioneer.** 1941

Whitney, Caspar. **Hawaiian America.** 1899

Wiest, Edward. **Agricultural Organization in the United States.** 1923